THE
2011 LSU
TIGERS:

UNDEFEATED SEC CHAMPIONS,
BCS CHAMPIONSHIP GAME,
& A COLLEGE FOOTBALL
LEGACY

Dan Fathow

MEGALODON ENTERTAINMENT, LLC.

Published by Megalodon Entertainment, LLC. (USA)
www.MegalodonEntertainment.com

First Printing: December 2011

Printed in the United States of America.

ISBN: 978-1-61589-030-9
ISBN-10: 1-61589-030-0

BULK INQUERIES:
Quantity discounts are available on bulk orders of this novel for educational, fund-raising, promotional, and special sales purposes.
For details, please contact www.MegalodonEntertainment.com

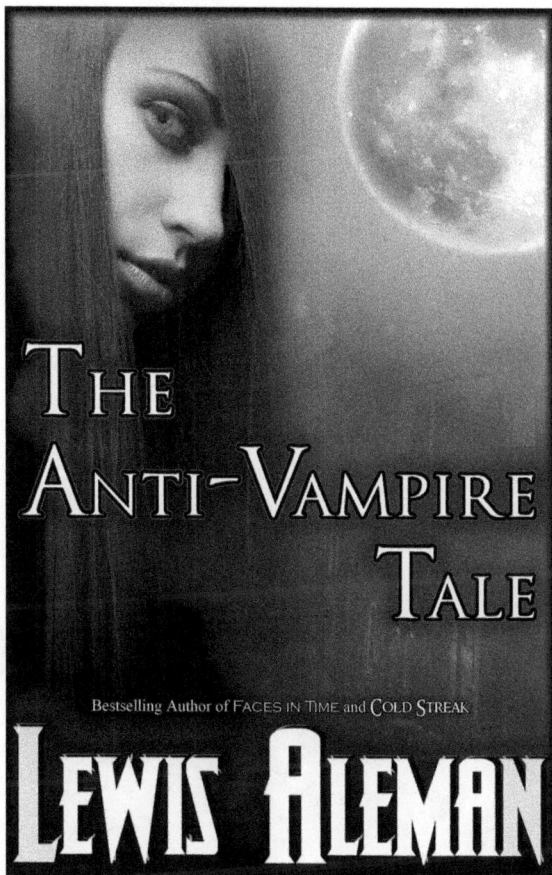

THE 2011 LSU TIGERS:

UNDEFEATED SEC CHAMPIONS, BCS CHAMPIONSHIP GAME, & A COLLEGE FOOTBALL LEGACY

Dan Fathow

TABLE OF CONTENTS

INTRODUCTION

Introduction:
Perfection &
Depth

Coming off an impressive 11-2 record in 2010, expectations were high for Les Miles and the Cotton Bowl Champion LSU Tigers in 2011, but few experts would have predicted an undefeated season, an SEC Championship, *and* a trip to the BCS Championship Game. And surely, hardly anyone would have foreseen the countless debates on whether the team was one of the best of all time.

The Striped Squad of Death Valley provided a lot of excitement for Tiger fans in 2011. A perfect regular season, the first in over 50 years for the team, was a thrilling ride. Over the course of the 12 regular season games and the SEC Championship Game, LSU outscored its opponents by an astonishing 363 points.

Not only did the LSU Tigers provide such a thrilling season, great stats, and a perfect record, but they did so while having a tough schedule, arguably one of the toughest in college football in 2011, and possibly even one of the hardest in history. Over the course of the year, LSU played and defeated 8 ranked teams, and 5 of those victories came on the road.

Now, while some people may question the validity of the BCS ranking system in the first place, it's hard to question the honor of ESPN *Game Day* selecting 4 of LSU's games to be showcased in 1 season. While people may argue about East or West Coast bias in sports reporting, no one is arguing that southern teams get a preference anywhere. For LSU to be put into the spotlight 4 times in 2011 by a national show whose profits are dependent on its choosing the most competitive college football games, it cements the credibility that the Tigers indeed had an amazingly tough schedule.

Besides these on-the-field challenges, LSU had more than its share of off-the-field conflicts. Before the season even began, 22 LSU players broke curfew, and some of them were involved in a controversial fight in a bar parking lot. The most worrisome of the allegations was that starting quarterback Jordan Jefferson kicked a young man in the head while he was already beaten down to the ground. That was a nightmare come to life for Les Miles: his team was disgraced for inappropriate behavior, and his starting quarterback was out indefinitely for fighting outside of a bar, possibly needing to serve jail time. And to top that off, it came just before the season opener against #3-ranked Oklahoma. Not only was it a huge setback, but the Tigers had very little time to adjust to it before meeting one of the best teams in the country on a national stage.

Not long after the bar fight debacle, 3 LSU players were suspended for possession of illegal synthetic marijuana. Those suspended were leading rusher, Spencer Ware; star defensive and special teams player, Tyrann Mathieu; and defensive end, Tharold Simon.

Despite these unfortunate events that could undermine even the strongest of locker rooms, the Tigers flourished. Their 2011 season is not just a story of dominating success, but one of focus and perseverance. With little time to prepare for his new role as a team leader, backup quarterback Jarrett Lee stepped up and performed like a first stringer, leading the Tigers to victory when they could easily have fallen apart under the pressure of embarrassing and costly off-field drama.

Depth is the word that is used the most often to describe the tremendous success of the 2011 LSU Tigers football team. When star running back Spencer Ware was out against Auburn, 4th-string Kenny Hilliard took charge and rushed for 65 yards and 2 touchdowns on 10 carries. That's only one example of LSU players rising to the occasion when called upon, finding a way to win every time. That's what makes a championship team. That's what makes an undefeated team. And, that's what makes a team one of the best of all time.

THE 2011 LSU TIGERS 15

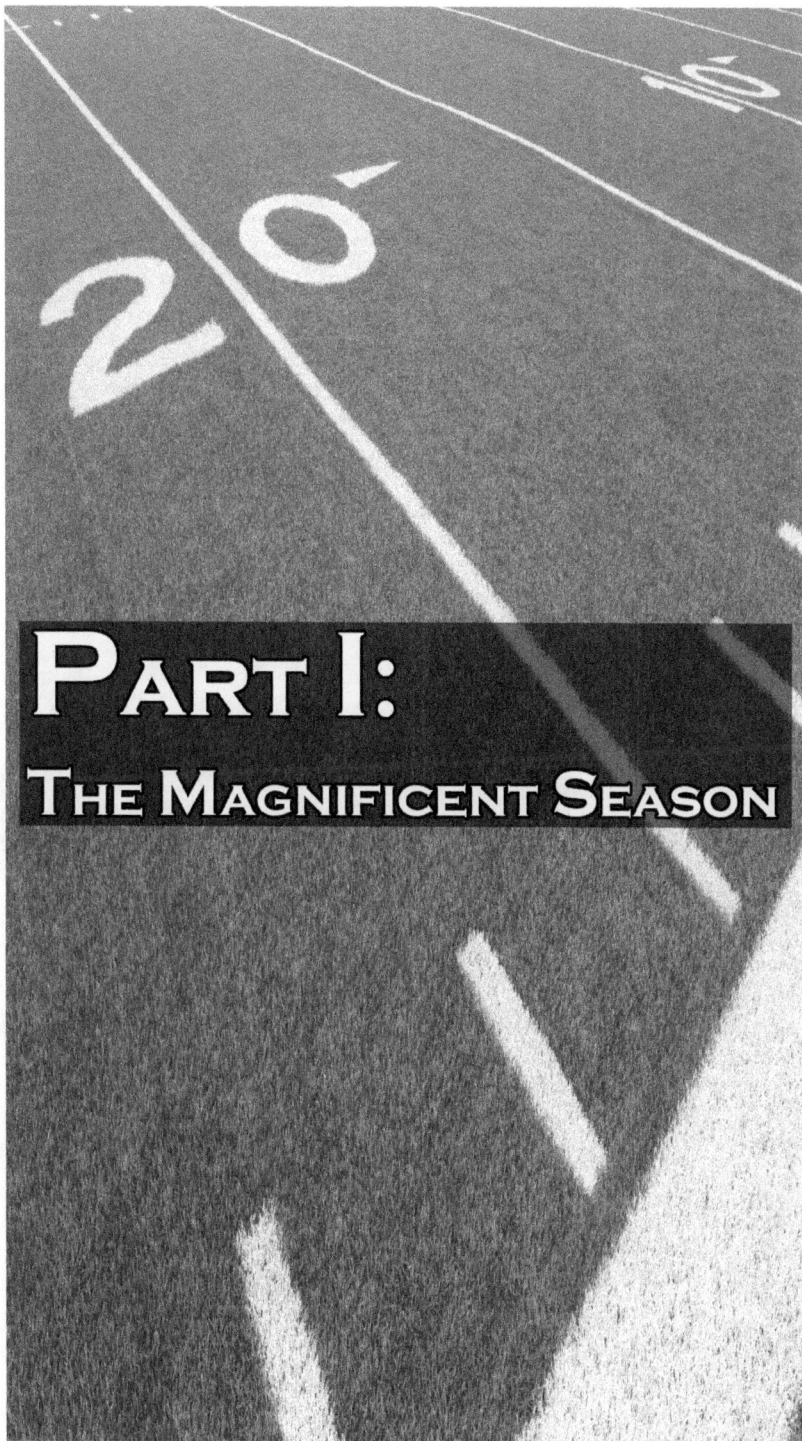

PART I:
THE MAGNIFICENT SEASON

GAME 1

September 3, 2011
Cowboys Stadium – Arlington, TX

Teams	1st	2nd	3rd	4th	Total
#3 Oregon	6	7	0	14	**27**
#4 LSU	3	13	14	10	**40**

GAME SUMMARY

The buzz going into the game was not so much that #3 Oregon was facing #4 LSU in a fantastic start to the college football season, but it was about whether LSU was going to implode in the wake of losing its star quarterback, Jordan Jefferson, to a senseless bar fight.

Like most of what happens in mainstream media, the focus was on the ridiculous drama. Lucky for us, what we got was some great, no-nonsense football from a focused LSU team, led by a determined backup quarterback, Jarrett Lee. Lee had a great start with a passing touchdown and no interceptions, leading the Tigers to a 13-point victory over a higher-ranked Oregon team.

Team Leaders

Passing

Jarrett Lee #12
98 Yards, 1 Touchdown, 0 Interceptions
(10/22, 45 Comp %)

Rushing

Spencer Ware #11
99 Yards on 26 Carries
3.8 Yards per Carry
1 Touchdown

Michael Ford #42
96 Yards on 14 Carries
6.9 Yards per Carry
2 Touchdowns

Receiving

Deangelo Peterson #19
62 Yards on 4 Receptions
15.5 Yards per Reception
0 Touchdowns

Rueben Randle #2
1 Touchdown Reception

Kicking

Drew Alleman
10 Points Total
2/2 Field Goals (44 & 32 Yards)
4/5 Extra Points

Interceptions

Tharold Simon #24
1 Interception

THE BOTTOM LINE

1 - 0

GAME 2

September 10, 2011
Tiger Stadium - Baton Rouge, LA

Teams	1st	2nd	3rd	4th	Total
Northwestern State	0	3	0	0	3
#2 LSU	7	21	14	7	49

GAME SUMMARY

After shocking a lot of the sports world with their 13-point victory over #3 Oregon the week before, LSU moved up in the rankings to #2. The Tigers had proven that they were not going to unravel facing their preseason adversity and that they were ready to compete against anyone.

Not many people gave Northwestern State much of a chance against the Tigers, but few would have predicted that LSU would have won by a margin of 46 points while playing 3rd-string quarterback Zach Mettenberger for part of the game. Jarrett Lee also had a great day. Both QBs had a touchdown, high completion percentages, and zero interceptions.

TEAM LEADERS

Passing

Jarrett Lee #12
133 Yards, 1 Touchdown, 0 Interceptions
(9/10, 90 Comp %)

Zach Mettenberger #8
92 Yards, 1 Touchdown, 0 Interceptions
(8/11, 73 Comp %)

Rushing

Michael Ford #42
72 Yards on 13 Carries
5.5 Yards per Carry
2 Touchdowns

Alfred Blue #4
53 Yards on 15 Carries
3.5 Yards per Carry
1 Touchdown

Spencer Ware #11
20 Yards on 6 Carries
3.3 Yards per Carry
2 Touchdowns

Receiving

Rueben Randle #2
121 Yards on 5 Receptions
24.2 Yards per Reception
0 Touchdowns

Odell Beckham #33
40 Yards on 5 Receptions

8 Yards per Reception
0 Touchdowns

Kadron Boone #86
28 Yards on 2 Receptions
14 Yards per Reception
1 Touchdown

Deangelo Peterson #19
9 Yards on 1 Receptions
9 Yards per Reception
1 Touchdowns

Kicking

Drew Alleman
7 Points Total
0/1 Field Goals
7/7 Extra Points

Interceptions

Michael Brockers #90
1 Interception

THE BOTTOM LINE

2 - 0

GAME 3

September 15, 2011
Davis Wade Stadium - Starkville, MS

Teams	1st	2nd	3rd	4th	Total
#25 Miss. St.	3	0	3	0	6
#3 LSU	3	3	3	10	19

GAME SUMMARY

To those who questioned LSU's early season success as just having a good game against #3 Oregon and getting a "gimme" win against Northwestern State, the 3rd game of the season was proof that the Tigers were a serious contender for the National Championship.

Mississippi State was ranked #25 at the time of the contest, and proved to be the 2nd ranked team that LSU beat soundly in just 3 games. The real story of the game was in the dominating performance given by LSU's defense against the SEC's most successful rushing attack. Going into the game, Mississippi State had an average of 321 rushing yards per game, which was #1 in the SEC and #6 in the entire FBS. The Tigers' D held Mississippi State to just 58 rushing yards, which was the fewest yards earned by the Bulldogs in 3 years.

This game validated LSU's #3 ranking to any disbelievers. The Tigers beat a ranked team by 13 points, while keeping them from scoring a single touchdown. That combination of offensive and defensive power made it clear that they were indeed contenders for the national title.

TEAM LEADERS

Passing

Jarrett Lee #12
213 Yards, 1 Touchdown, 1 Interception
(21/27, 78 Comp %)

Rushing

Spencer Ware #11
107 Yards on 22 Carries
4.9 Yards per Carry
0 Touchdowns

Michael Ford #42
50 Yards on 13 Carries
3.8 Yards per Carry
0 Touchdowns

Receiving

Rueben Randle #2
98 Yards on 6 Receptions
16.3 Yards per Reception
1 Touchdown

Odell Beckham #33
61 Yards on 8 Receptions
7.6 Yards per Reception
0 Touchdowns

Kicking

Drew Alleman
13 Points Total
4/4 Field Goals, (21, 42, 41, & 29 Yards)
1/1 Extra Points

Interceptions

Morris Claiborne #17
1 Interception

THE BOTTOM LINE

3 - 0

GAME 4

September 24, 2011
Mountaineer Field - Morgantown, WV

Teams	1st	2nd	3rd	4th	Total
#16 W Virginia	0	7	14	0	21
#2 LSU	13	14	7	13	47

GAME SUMMARY

Game 4 of the 2011 season was the 3rd time that the Tigers faced a ranked team, and it became their 3rd victory against ranked teams. A 4-0 overall record with a 3-0 record against Top-25 ranked teams is arguably one of the most impressive 4-game starts in recent memory, if not collegiate football history.

After beating West Virginia, the 16th-ranked team in the country by a staggering 26 points, LSU coach Les Miles said:

"Our guys seem to answer the bell, enjoy a competitive environment. I feel comfortable going on the road and playing with this team. I think if we continue to improve, continue to do the things we're capable of, somewhere down the road, we'll stake a claim on something important."

(Andrea Adelson, *Big East Blog*, *http://espn.go.com/blog/bigeast/post/_/id/24098/lsu-withstands-rally-answers-challenge*)

This performance made a strong argument that the #2-ranked Tigers should replace Oklahoma as the top-ranked team in the country.

TEAM LEADERS

Passing

Jarrett Lee #12
180 Yards, 3 Touchdown, 0 Interceptions
(16/28, 57 Comp %)

Rushing

Spencer Ware #11
92 Yards on 23 Carries
4.0 Yards per Carry
0 Touchdowns

Michael Ford #42
82 Yards on 12 Carries
6.8 Yards per Carry
2 Touchdowns

Alfred Blue #4
2 Yards on 21 Carries
10.5 Yards per Carry
1 Touchdown

Receiving

Odell Beckham #33

82 Yards on 2 Receptions
41 Yards per Reception
1 Touchdown

Rueben Randle #2
53 Yards on 6 Receptions
8.8 Yards per Reception
1 Touchdown

Kicking

Drew Alleman
5 Points Total
0/1 Field Goals
5/5 Extra Points

Interceptions

Brandon Taylor #18
1 Interception

Tyrann Mathieu #7
1 Interception

THE BOTTOM LINE

4 - 0

GAME 5

October 1, 2011
Tiger Stadium – Baton Rouge, LA

Teams	1st	2nd	3rd	4th	Total
Kentucky	0	0	0	7	7
#1 LSU	7	7	14	7	**35**

GAME SUMMARY

The impressive performance put up by LSU in the previous week was enough to get the Tigers the #1 ranking for the first time this season. And, it was an honor that the team would maintain for the rest of the season, despite their challenging schedule.

The University of Kentucky came into this game with an even 2-2 record, and they were really given no chance to win this game without providing one of the biggest upsets of the year.

The big story of the game had little to do with LSU's performance but in the return of Jordan Jefferson from his suspension for his involvement in a bar parking lot fight before the season began.

Jefferson did not start the game but only came on in relief of Jarrett Lee. There were audible boos as Jefferson took the field in Tiger Stadium for the first time in the season, and there are 2 plausible but very different reasons for this fan reaction:

1. The obvious: fans were indeed booing Jefferson because they were disgusted with his behavior and did not want an athlete on their beloved team who allegedly kicked a man in the head when he was knocked down on the ground. This is the most obvious possibility and could easily have been the case for some, if not most, of the unhappy fans.

2. The fans may not have so much been booing out of disapproval or disdain for Jefferson; they may have simply been booing at the decision to take Jarrett Lee out of the game. Jarrett Lee had already become a hero for LSU fans by stepping up from backup duty to lead the LSU Tigers to victory in 4 straight games, including 3 against Top-25 ranked teams, especially the season opener against #3 Oregon.

When the bar fight debacle happened, many LSU fans were worried that the 2011 season would already be a wash without Jordan Jefferson. What fan wouldn't appreciate a backup who essentially not only saved their team from an embarrassing and dismal season but lead them to become #1 in the country?

LSU became #1 without the services of Jordan Jefferson. The Tigers became the best in the country without Jefferson's help at all. What more could Jarrett Lee do to deserve the starting quarterback position? You can't get any better than undefeated, especially against the competition that Lee and the Tigers had faced in the first 4 games of 2011. It's very understandable that many fans felt Lee had earned his position under extremely trying circumstances and without the time needed to properly prepare. When a player does so much for a team, especially when many experts were predicting LSU to flounder, he earns the loyalty and respect of the fans. When a respected player is asked to sit the bench, fans become upset. When a respected player is asked to sit the bench for another player who jeopardized the team's entire season, fans boo. It's about respect for the backup underdog who led the team to the top spot in all of college football; it's not about hate or disrespect.

In all honesty, there were certainly #1 and #2 going on in the stands. The question is: were there more boos for respect for Lee or dislike of Jefferson? That's a question we may never know the answer to. However, the fans were certainly cheering at a final score of 35-7.

TEAM LEADERS

Passing

Jarrett Lee #12
169 Yards, 1 Touchdown, 0 Interceptions
(8/21, 38 Comp %)

Jordan Jefferson #9
(no passing, just running plays in this game)

Rushing

Alfred Blue #4
72 Yards on 16 Carries
4.5 Yards per Carry
1 Touchdown

Terrence Magee #14
38 Yards on 12 Carries

3.2 Yards per Carry
1 Touchdown

Jordan Jefferson #9
29 Yards on 4 Carries
7.3 Yards per Carry
1 Touchdown

Receiving

Odell Beckham #33
75 Yards on 3 Receptions
25 Yards per Reception
1 Touchdown

Rueben Randle #2
37 Yards on 1 Reception
37 Yards per Reception
0 Touchdowns

Kicking

Drew Alleman
5 Points Total
0/0 Field Goals
5/5 Extra Points

Interceptions

None

Tyrann Mathieu #7
1 Interception

THE BOTTOM LINE

5 - 0

GAME 6

October 8, 2011
Tiger Stadium – Baton Rouge, LA

Teams	1st	2nd	3rd	4th	Total
#17 Florida	0	3	8	0	**11**
#1 LSU	14	10	3	14	**41**

GAME SUMMARY

The 6th game of the season was also the 4th game in which LSU faced a ranked opponent in the #17 Florida Gators. The Gators came into the game with a 4-1 record, and their only loss came at the hands of the then #3-ranked Alabama Crimson Tide.

Some may argue that Florida was over-ranked at #17. The Gators did go on to lose to all 5 ranked teams they played in 2011, and they also lost to unranked Florida State to close out the regular season at an even 6-6. So, there seems to be some truth that Florida was indeed over-ranked heading into Game 6.

LSU opened the game with taking a 14-0 lead in the 1st quarter. From that point on, the Tigers kept a commanding lead, never allowing the Gators to close the gap enough to make this a close game.

Jordan Jefferson did take a few more snaps, passing for a touchdown and keeping a slightly higher completion percentage than Jarrett Lee. Neither QB threw an interception in this impressive victory.

TEAM LEADERS

Passing

Jarrett Lee #12
154 Yards, 1 Touchdown, 0 Interceptions
(7-10, 70 Comp %)

Jordan Jefferson #9
61 Yards, 1 Touchdown, 0 Interceptions
(3-4, 75 Comp %)

Rushing

Spencer Ware #11
109 yards on 24 Carries
2 Touchdowns

Alfred Blue #4
70 Yards on 14 Carries
5.0 Yards per Carry
1 Touchdown

Receiving

Rueben Randle #2
127 Yards on 4 Receptions
1 Touchdown

Russell Shepard #10
41 Yards on 2 Receptions
0 Touchdowns

Mitch Joseph #83
1 Touchdown Reception (2 Yards)

Kicking

Drew Alleman
11 Points Total
2/2 Field Goals, (35 & 23 Yards)
5/5 Extra Points

Interceptions

Brandon Taylor #18
1 Interception

Tyrann Mathieu #7
1 Interception

THE BOTTOM LINE

6 - 0

GAME 7

October 15, 2011
Neyland Stadium – Knoxville, TN

Teams	1st	2nd	3rd	4th	Total
Tennessee	0	7	0	0	7
#1 LSU	0	17	7	14	**38**

GAME SUMMARY

The week before, LSU beat Florida by 30 points. In Game 7, the Tigers beat Tennessee by 31 points. This is the part of the season when LSU was putting up some very impressive offensive numbers to match their well-respected defense.

Once again Lee and Jefferson were both taking snaps for the Tigers. Lee's numbers were much more impressive than Jefferson's in this game, having thrown for 3 touchdowns with 0 interceptions. Jefferson performed as more of a rusher than a QB, running for 73 yards and 1 touchdown.

TEAM LEADERS

Passing

Jarrett Lee #12
138 Yards, 3 Touchdowns, 0 Interceptions
(13-17, 76.5 Comp %)

Jordan Jefferson #9
8 Yards, 0 Touchdown, 0 Interceptions
(1-3, 33.3 Comp %)

Rushing

Spencer Ware #11
80 yards on 23 Carries
1 Touchdown

Jordan Jefferson #9
73 Yards on 14 Carries
1 Touchdown

Receiving

Rueben Randle #2
86 Yards on 5 Receptions
17.2 Yards per Reception
1 Touchdown

Odell Beckham #33
24 Yards on 4 Receptions
6 Yards per Reception
0 Touchdowns

Russell Shepard #10
14 Yards on 1 Receptions
14 Yards per Reception
1 Touchdown

Spencer Ware #11
13 Yards on 1 Carries
13 Yards per Carry
1 Touchdown

Kicking

Drew Alleman
8 Points Total
1/1 Field Goals, 36 Yards
5/5 Extra Points

Interceptions

Morris Claiborne #17
1 Interception

Eric Reid #1
1 Interception

THE BOTTOM LINE

7 - 0

GAME 8

October 22, 2011
Tiger Stadium – Baton Rouge, LA

Teams	1st	2nd	3rd	4th	Total
#20 Auburn	3	0	0	7	**10**
#1 LSU	7	14	21	3	**45**

GAME SUMMARY

E ven though #20 Auburn came into the game with a 5-2 record, having lost to #10 Arkansas and unranked Clemson, some thought Auburn had the potential to provide LSU with their hardest test of the year. After all, Auburn had indeed beaten #10 South Carolina. Before losing to Auburn, South Carolina were undefeated, and they would go on to finish their season with an impressive 10-2 record. So, they had already beaten a great team. Auburn was no pushover.

However, LSU did push them over, defeating the Auburn Tigers by a whopping 35 points. This made the 3rd week in a row that LSU defeated their opponent by 30 or more points, and 2 of those opponents were ranked teams. These large-margin victories against ranked teams proved LSU's dominance and justified their #1 ranking.

The big news of the game was that LSU was suffering from another huge off-field setback. Due to a violation of the school's drug policy, specifically synthetic marijuana, 3 LSU players were suspended from the game including the team's leading rusher, Spencer Ware; playmaker and Heisman darkhorse, Tyrann Mathieu; and Tharold Simon, defensive back. However, the Tigers overcame the off-field setback just as they had at the start of the season with the bar fight. The team stayed focused, determined, and not only won, but won big.

Just as Jarrett Lee stepped up and performed well when Jordan Jefferson was suspended, Kenny Hilliard picked up the slack from suspended Spencer Ware, rushing for 2 touchdowns and averaging 6.5 yards per carry.

TEAM LEADERS

Passing

Jarrett Lee #12
165 Yards, 2 Touchdowns, 0 Interceptions
(14-20, 70 Comp %)

Jordan Jefferson #9
54 Yards, 1 Touchdowns, 0 Interceptions
(2-3, 66.6 Comp %)

Rushing

Michael Ford #42
82 Yards on 12 Carries
6.8 Yards per Carry
0 Touchdowns

Kenny Hilliard #27
65 yards on 10 Carries
2 Touchdowns

Receiving

Rueben Randle #2
106 Yards on 5 Receptions
2 Touchdowns

Russell Shepard #10
1 Receiving Touchdown

Kicking

Drew Alleman
9 Points Total
1/1 Field Goals, 36 Yards
3/3 Extra Points

Interceptions

Ron Brooks #13
1 Interception Returned for a 28-Yard Touchdown

THE BOTTOM LINE

8 - 0

GAME 9

November 5, 2011
Bryant-Denny Stadium – Tuscaloosa, AL

Teams	1st	2nd	3rd	4th	OT	Total
#2 Alabama	0	3	3	0	0	**6**
#1 LSU	0	3	0	3	3	**9**

GAME SUMMARY

Dubbed *The Game of the Century* by the sports media, the undefeated, #1-ranked LSU Tigers met the undefeated, #2-ranked Alabama Crimson Tide on Saturday November 5, 2011 at 7:00 p.m.

Adding to the media frenzy was that not only were #1 and #2 meeting, guaranteeing an end to someone's perfect season, but LSU was facing off against its longtime rival whose head coach is none other than The Tiger's former head honcho, Nick Saban. Everything about the game had high-profile, smash-mouth, grudge-match football written all over it.

As usual, the media's practice of hyping something up to epicly ridiculous proportions left many viewers feeling disappointed when they finally watched the game. The game was a defensive contest, which is certainly out of style in 2011, a time when 3 different NFL quarterbacks were poised to shatter the all-time season passing record (which was indeed accomplished by Drew Brees about 8 weeks later). With that kind of an exciting, high-scoring football atmosphere, it was indeed hard to appreciate a 9-6 defensive war as "the game of the century," especially when Alabama's poor kicking had more to do with their loss than the Tiger's offense.

Being that these 2 teams would soon have their rematch in the national championship, there was definitely validity to *some* of the hype. In the media's defense, LSU and Alabama were certainly the 2 best teams in college football (their end of year records proved that) at the time, and it should have been the game of the year, if not the game of the decade. The game of the century is another story.

TEAM LEADERS

Passing

Jordan Jefferson #9
168 Yards, 1 Touchdowns, 0 Interceptions
(8-14, 57 Comp %)

Jarrett Lee #12
15 Yards, 1 Touchdowns, 0 Interceptions
(2-4, 50 Comp %)

Rushing

Michael Ford #42
119 Yards on 9 Carries
13.2 Yards per Carry
2 Touchdowns

Receiving

Russell Shepard #10
39 Yards on 2 Receptions
19.5 Yards per Reception
0 Touchdowns

Kicking

Drew Alleman
9 Points Total (including the game winning FG in OT)
3/3 Field Goals, (19, 30, & 25 Yards)
0/0 Extra Points
*Alleman scored all of the Tigers points in this game

Interceptions

Morris Claiborne #17
1 Interception

Eric Reid #1
1 Interception

THE BOTTOM LINE

9 - 0

GAME 10

November 12, 2011
Tiger Stadium – Baton Rouge, LA

Teams	1st	2nd	3rd	4th	Total
W. Kentucky	7	0	2	0	**9**
#1 LSU	7	7	14	14	**42**

GAME SUMMARY

After narrowly beating #2 Alabama by a margin of 3 points, LSU immediately returned to their practice of pounding teams in 30+ point victories, starting with their routing of W Kentucky, defeating them by 33 points.

W Kentucky was 5-4 coming into the game, and what was more impressive was that they were on a 5-game winning streak after opening the season with 4 straight losses. Despite their string of victories, W Kentucky was not expected to be much of a challenge for LSU, as the 42-9 Tigers victory proved.

Jordan Jefferson was taking more snaps than Jarrett Lee, throwing less interceptions, and putting up a better completion percentage.

TEAM LEADERS

Passing

Jordan Jefferson #9
67 Yards, 0 Touchdowns, 0 Interceptions
(6-10, 60 Comp %)

Jarrett Lee #12
24 Yards, 0 Touchdowns, 2 Interceptions
(3-7, 43 Comp %)

Rushing

Alfred Blue #4
72 Yards on 11 Carries
6.5 Yards per Carry
0 Touchdown

Kenny Hilliard #27
2 Touchdowns

Receiving

Reuben Randle #2
76 Yards on 3 Receptions
25.3 Yards per Reception
1 Touchdowns

Kicking

Drew Alleman
6 Points Total
0/0 Field Goals
6/6 Extra Points

Interceptions

Tahj Jones #58
1 Interception

THE BOTTOM LINE

10 - 0

GAME 11

November 19, 2011
Vaught-Hemingway Stadium – Oxford, MS

Teams	1st	2nd	3rd	4th	Total
Ole Miss	0	3	0	0	3
#1 LSU	21	14	14	3	52

GAME SUMMARY

Ole Miss vs. LSU is a big game in Baton Rouge or Oxford in any year, regardless of either team's record or the significance the game may have on rankings or bowl appearances. It's a regional rivalry that always generates heat, and the #1 ranked Tigers facing the 2-8 Rebels was no exception.

LSU crushed Ole Miss as expected, winning all 4 quarters easily, starting the 1st quarter 21-0, and finishing with an impressive score of 52-3. In fact, the score was so impressive that some wondered if it was a case of running up the scoreboard needlessly and in bad taste. The other side of that argument is that there is no practice like actually playing in a game, and when you're looking at going to the National Championship, you better get in all the real-game practice you can. In addition to that, scoring is important to maintain or improve a team's ranking in the BCS system.

TEAM LEADERS

Passing

Jordan Jefferson #9
88 Yards, 1 Touchdowns, 0 Interceptions
(7-7, 100 Comp %)

Jarrett Lee #12
17 Yards, 0 Touchdowns, 0 Interceptions
(1-1, 100 Comp %)

Rushing

Alfred Blue
74 yards on 4 Carries
18.5 Yards per Carry
0 Touchdowns

Spencer Ware #11
70 yards on 10 Carries
7 Yards per Carry
1 Touchdown

Kenny Hilliard #27
1 Touchdown

James Stampley
1 Touchdown

Receiving

Deangelo Peterson #19
28 Yards on 2 Receptions
14 Yards per Reception
0 Touchdowns

Rueben Randle #2
22 Yards on 1 Reception
1 Touchdown

Kicking

Drew Alleman
10 Points Total
1/1 Field Goals (29 Yards)
7/7 Extra Points

Interceptions

Ron Brooks #13
1 Interception Returned for a 46-Yard Touchdown

THE BOTTOM LINE

11 - 0

GAME 12

November 25, 2011
Tiger Stadium – Baton Rouge, LA

Teams	1st	2nd	3rd	4th	Total
#3 Arkansas	0	14	3	0	**17**
#1 LSU	0	21	3	17	**41**

GAME SUMMARY

For the 7th time this season, LSU faced a ranked opponent in #3 Arkansas. It also made the 3rd time that LSU had to play a team ranked in the Top 3 (Oregan #3, Alabama #2, and Arkansas #3). One could easily argue that with this victory, LSU had already played and won 3 games that were the caliber of a BCS Title Game.

Further showing how much better they were than any other team in college football, LSU routed the #3 team in the country by a powerful 24 points.

What was unusual about this game is that in the 2nd quarter, the Tigers found themselves down by 14 points. The tide really turned around when big-play-maker Tyrann Mathieu returned a punt 92-yards for a touchdown to tie the game at 14-14. Part of what makes a legendary team is not just the ability to pound opponents when you have the lead, but the heart that it takes to come back from being down by 2 touchdowns to win by 24 points. That's impressive against any opponent, and it's especially awe-inspiring against the #3 Razorbacks.

The most controversial moment of the game came after the 4th quarter ended and did not involve a single player on either team. At the post-game handshake, Arkansas coach Bobby Petrino abruptly turned away from LSU coach Les Miles, rudely snubbing him publicly. While that loss meant that his #3 Hogs had zero chance of being selected to meet LSU in the title game, that kind of behavior from a collegiate head coach is unacceptable. Coach Petrino's disappointment is understandable, and his work with the 10-2 Hogs is admirable. However, there is no excuse for his behavior, and his lack of sportsmanship is deplorable. Hostile, sore-loser behavior is embarrassing on a playground team; it's unfathomable from a head coach representing a great university while earning a 7-figure salary.

TEAM LEADERS

Passing

Jordan Jefferson #9
208 Yards, 1 Touchdowns, 1 Interceptions
(18/29, 62 Comp %)

Rushing

Kenny Hilliard #27
102 Yards on 19 Carries
5.4 Yards per Carry
1 Touchdown

Michael Ford #42
96 Yards on 11 Carries
8.7 Yards per Carry
0 Touchdowns

The 2011 LSU Tigers 65

Jordan Jefferson #9
1 Rushing Touchdown

Spencer Ware #11
1 Rushing Touchdown

Receiving

Reuben Randle #2
76 Yards on 3 Receptions
25.3 Yards per Reception
0 Touchdowns

Odell Beckham #33
27 Yards on 3 Receptions
25.3 Yards per Reception
0 Touchdowns

Russell Shepard #10
1 Receiving Touchdown

Kicking

Drew Alleman
11 Points Total
2/2 Field Goals (37 & 21 Yards)
5/5 Extra Points

Interceptions

Morris Claiborne #17
1 Interception

THE BOTTOM LINE

12 - 0

GAME 13

December 3, 2011
Georgia Dome – Atlanta, GA

Teams	1st	2nd	3rd	4th	Total
#14 Georgia	10	0	0	0	**10**
#1 LSU	0	7	21	14	**42**

GAME SUMMARY

Despite a terrible performance from quarterback Jordan Jefferson, the LSU Tigers managed to slaughter the Georgia Bulldogs 42-10.

The one thing that no one could stop talking about was the amazingly poor offensive effort from LSU in the first half. Failing to get a single first down in the first half of an SEC Championship Game, the LSU Tigers looked like a distinctively different and weaker team than anyone had seen all year long.

Ironically, the strong criticism of this poor performance is what can prove the caliber of this LSU team. Coming back to win by 32 points against a 10-and-2, SEC East Champ Georgia team after being down 10-0 in the first quarter and not having moved the down markers a single time in the first half, proves the quality of the 2011 Tigers. Only a team with tremendous determination and depth could come back from that to win by so much. For example, the offense can't put up any numbers on the scoreboard, so Matthieu does it on a punt return. LSU is down 10 points in the 1st Quarter because Quarterback Jordan Jefferson is putting up some of the worst numbers in his career, so the defense steps up and goose-eggs Georgia for the rest of the game. Also, keep in mind that Georgia was on a 10-game winning streak coming into the championship game.

A good team relies on its particular strength to carry them to victory. A great team has enough depth at every position to fight back and win even when that particular strength is floundering. LSU proved that time and again in 2011 with its on and off the field challenges.

How do you win when you're down 10-7 in the 1st half, when your offense has put up a total of 12 yards on 10 plays, and you haven't gotten a single first down? Essentially, you have to watch this game to learn how. You also have to stay focused and never give up. In 2011, LSU had plenty of practice with focusing on playing football and not being distracted or intimidated by setbacks. LSU's off-the-field setbacks were enough to derail any team from having a good year, much less a great one, and even less one of the greatest of all time. Perhaps, these setbacks earlier in the year proved to be practice for staying focused and coming back in this very game.

Coming back to win in an SEC championship game instills a lot of confidence among fans. However, it is undeniable that Jordan Jefferson's poor 5-of-13 for 30 yards passing performance is a huge concern for the Tigers heading into one of the most hyped-up BCS Championship Games in recent memory. Simply put, he'll have to do much better than that to beat the 2nd-rated college football team in the country, a team that in the regular season, LSU only defeated by a field goal in overtime. Incidentally, Jefferson was 8-of-14 for 168 yards in that narrow, 3-point victory.

TEAM LEADERS

Passing

Jordan Jefferson #9
30 Yards, 1 Touchdown, 0 Interceptions
(5/13, 38 Comp %)

Rushing

Alfred Blue #4
94 Yards on 8 Carries
11.8 Yards per Carry
1 Touchdown

Kenny Hilliard #27
72 Yards on 8 Carries
9 Yards per Carry
2 Touchdowns

Michael Ford #42
34 Yards on 6 Carries
5.7 Yards per Carry
0 Touchdowns

Receiving

Reuben Randle #2
15 Yards on 2 Receptions
7.5 Yards per Reception
0 Touchdowns

Kenny Hilliard #27
1 Receiving Touchdown (8 yards)

Kicking

Drew Alleman
6 Points Total

DAN FATHOW 70

0/0 Field Goals
6/6 Extra Points

Interceptions

Morris Claiborne #17
1 Interception Returned for a 45-Yard Touchdown

Tharold Simon #24
1 Interception

THE BOTTOM LINE

13 - 0

SEC CHAMPIONS

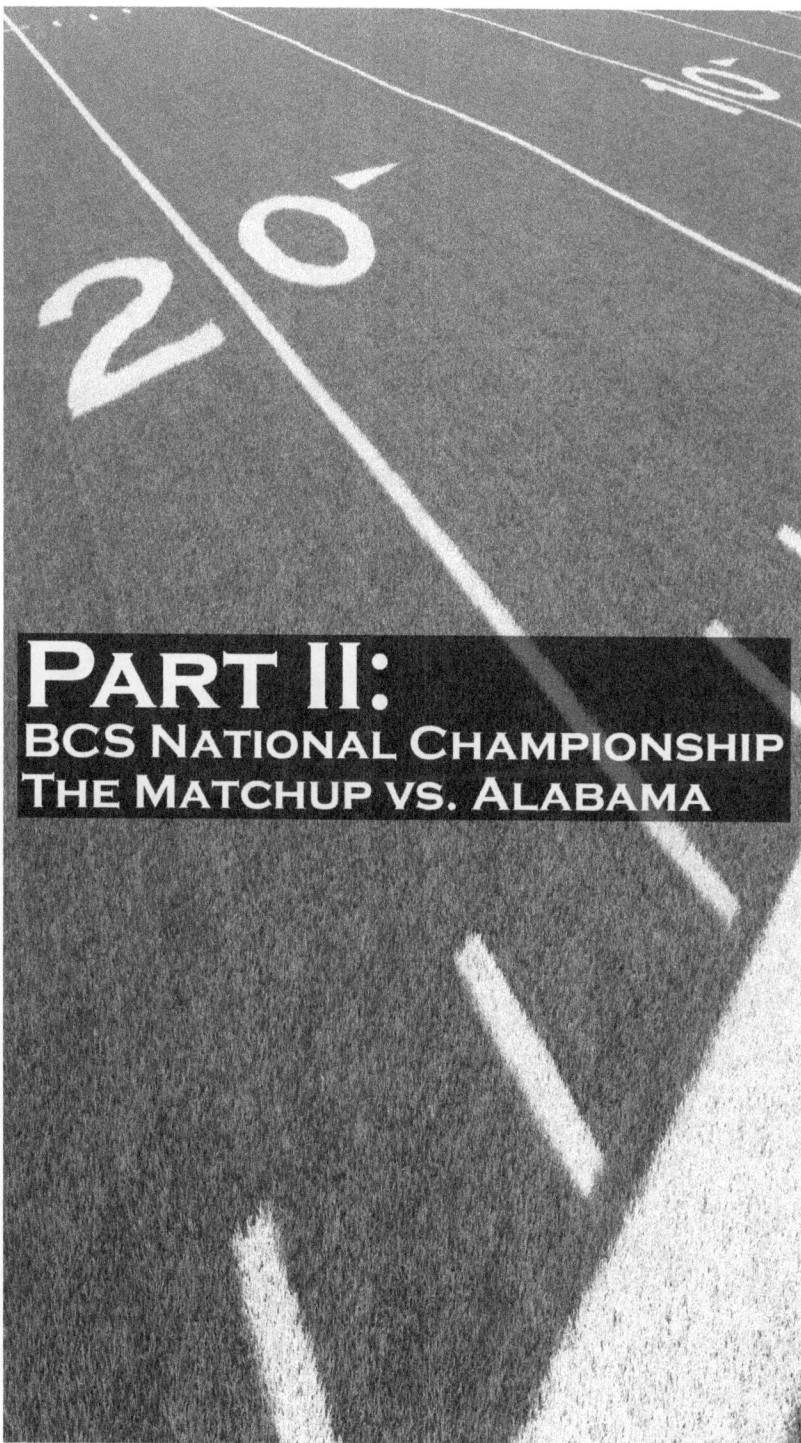

PART II:
BCS NATIONAL CHAMPIONSHIP
THE MATCHUP VS. ALABAMA

N o sports discussion should ever begin without statistics. Facts are the only valid form of debate, so let's begin by looking at the record of LSU's opponent:

2011 ALABAMA CRIMSON TIDE

Opponent	W/L	Score	Record to Date	Date
Kent State	W	48-07	1-0	09/03/11
#23 Penn State	W	27-11	2-0	09/10/11
North Texas	W	41-00	3-0	09/17/11
#14 Arkansas	W	38-14	4-0	09/24/11
#12 Florida	W	38-10	5-0	10/01/11
Vanderbilt	W	34-00	6-0	10/08/11
Ole Miss	W	52-07	7-0	10/15/11
Tennessee	W	37-6	8-0	10/22/11
#1 LSU	*L*	*09-06*	*8-1*	*11/05/11*
Mississippi State	W	24-07	9-1	11/12/11
Georgia Southern	W	45-21	10-1	11/19/11
#24 Auburn	W	42-14	11-1	11/26/11

Part of the dilemma in comparing two college football teams by their season statistics is the huge differences in schedule difficulty. For example, scoring 50 points against an unranked team is *significantly* easier than scoring 50 points against a Top-10 team. Therefore, when comparing the win/loss record and total points scored for a team, it is essential to look at the level of competition under which these stats were earned. Simply put, you want to compare apples to apples and oranges to oranges. With that in mind, here are some side-by-side comparisons between LSU and the Crimson Tide in an effort to see who was the better team while facing similar competition in 2011:

SIDE BY SIDE POINTS SCORED PER GAME

(The SEC Championship Game vs. Georgia has been shown in the 2nd column to show LSU's true season statistics. But, it's been left off the far right column record to give a fair 12-game comparison, because Alabama did not play a 13th game heading into the BCS Championship.)

GAME	LSU	ALA	LSU in 12
1	40	48	40
2	49	27	49
3	19	41	19
4	47	38	47
5	35	38	35
6	41	34	41
7	38	52	38
8	45	37	45
9	9	6	9
10	42	24	42
11	52	45	52
12	41	42	41
13	42		
	500	432	458

In the points scored category, LSU is the winner having scored 26 more points than Alabama. While that may not seem that it's such a large margin over the course of 12 games, it's still 2.16 more points per game, and you only need to lead by 1 to win. However, it's no denying that the teams are closely matched, even though LSU has an edge in scoring.

WINNER: LSU

Just as important as points scored are points allowed. Even if a team scores 100 points per game, they can lose every contest if they allow 101 points per game. So, here are those numbers:

SIDE BY SIDE POINTS ALLOWED PER GAME

(The SEC Championship Game vs. Georgia has been shown in the 2nd column to show LSU's true season statistics. But, it's been left off the far right column record to give a fair 12-game comparison, because Alabama did not play a 13th game heading into the BCS Championship.)

GAME	LSU Opponents	LSU Opp in 12	ALA Opponents
1	27	27	7
2	3	3	11
3	6	6	0
4	21	21	14
5	7	7	10
6	11	11	0
7	7	7	7
8	10	10	6
9	6	6	9
10	9	9	7
11	3	3	21
12	17	17	14
13	10		
	137	127	106

On Points Allowed per game, Alabama has the edge with allowing 21 less points over the course of 12 games.

AVERAGE POINTS ALLOWED PER GAME

Alabama – 8.873
LSU – 10.58

So, LSU allowed an average of 1.5 more points per game than Alabama.

WINNER: Alabama

However, this is where things get interesting. LSU scored an average of 2.16 more points per game than Alabama, while Alabama allowed 1.5 less points per game than LSU. This would mean that per game, LSU is ahead of Alabama by an average of *0.66 points per game.*

Overall Points Scored/Allowed WINNER: LSU

As said before, comparing the season stats is convoluted by the differences in the level of competition. So, here is a chart comparing LSU's and Alabama's performance when they played the same opponents.

Opponent	LSU	LSU OPP	LSU DATE	ALA	ALA OPP	ALA Date
Florida	41	11	8-Oct	38	10	1-Oct
Arkansas	41	17	25-Nov	38	14	24-Sep
Ole Miss	52	3	19-Nov	52	7	15-Oct
Tennessee	38	7	15-Oct	37	6	22-Oct
Miss State	19	6	15-Sep	24	7	12-Nov
Auburn	45	10	22-Oct	42	14	26-Nov
	236	**54**		**231**	**58**	

When playing the same opponents, LSU clearly played better than Alabama in 2011. Here is the breakdown:

Against the same 6 opponents in 2011:

LSU scored 236 points and only allowed 54 points, for an average margin of victory of **30.33 points per game.**

Alabama scored 231 points and only allowed 58 points, for an average margin of victory of **28.83 points per game.**

So, while the teams are still closely matched, LSU scored more points and allowed less points than Alabama while playing against the same teams. Alabama loses in both categories when comparing apples to apples.

Statistically speaking, LSU beat the same opponents by 1.5 more points per game than Alabama did. A half a field goal may not seem like much, but it's enough to win.

Points Scored/Allowed Against the Same Opponents WINNER: LSU

MOMENTUM, ADVANTAGES, & MINUTIAE

WEAR & TEAR

LSU will have played 13 games going into the BCS Title Game on January 9, 2011, and they will have last played against Georgia in the SEC Championship on December 3rd.

Alabama will have only played 12 games going into the BCS Title Game on January 9, 2011, and they will have last played against Auburn on November 26th.

One has to question the fairness of an undefeated #1 Ranked team having to play 13 games to get into the national championship while a #2 ranked team with 1 loss waltzes in after only having played 12 games. There are many problems that have been well documented with the BCS ranking/bowl system, but this particular set of circumstances is ridiculous and inexcusable. In the NFL, the top ranked team gets a bye in the playoffs. In 2011 in the BCS, the top-ranked team apparently has to play an ***EXTRA*** game to get to the championship. There is no logic or justification for this.

Fairness and logic aside, what does this mean in relation to the BCS Championship Game?

LSU has played one more game than Alabama, having put their players through more wear and tear.

Advantage: Alabama

TIME OFF - RUST FACTOR VS REST FACTOR

Alabama will have had 44 days off compared to LSU's 37 Days off. So, Alabama has had one more week off than LSU. More time off is not always a good thing. Whether the bye week in the NFL is beneficial or harmful has long been a debate among fans and commentators.

On advancednflstats.com, Denis O'Regan put together one of the best studies on this issue. After crunching a ton of numbers that are a bit irrelevant to this college football discussion, he came up with a conclusion that may be very relevant to the BCS Championship Game:

"Conclusion.

Favoured teams going on the road after a bye week appear to overperform by almost a field goal. This effect is largely absent in all other types of matchups."

(Denis O'Regan - Writer, Ed Anthony – Editor,
October 31, 2009
http://community.advancednflstats.com/2009/10/bye-weeks.html)

Okay, so that's an in-depth analysis of NFL teams' performances following a bye week. What does that have to do with the BCS Championship Game? Well, maybe nothing. Even if statistics are very strongly against something from happening in the sports world, there is a first time for everything, and there are no statistics that can prevent an athlete or a team to win in an underdog position. This very fact is probably what keeps us watching sports year after year. The chance that heart, determination, and hard work can make a champion out of someone that the world underestimated. And, by the same token, a tremendously talented team can lose to anyone if they grow overconfident, complacent, or take their opponent too lightly.

Okay, okay, so that's enough waxing poetic about the valor of sports. What does Mr. O'Regan's study mean for the BCS Championship Game?

Depending on where you look, LSU is favored to win between 1-1.5 points. There are even a few sources that are favoring Alabama to win by 1. Even though LSU is playing a near-home game in the Superdome in New Orleans, about 80 miles from Tiger Stadium, Alabama is definitely the road team in this scenario having to travel across two states and play in front of an LSU home crowd. If O'Regan's statistics hold true in the BCS title game, Alabama wins by 1.5 - 4 points.

Advantage: Alabama

4 College Football Factors that might skew the NFL bye-week statistics:

1-College students have finals and other end of the semester concerns to worry about in the time between the end of the regular season and the championship game. Pro athletes don't have this problem.

2-Most pro football players live in the cities where their teams are located. Many college players do not live in the same city as their college, and in some instances, not even the same state. So, visiting family during the holidays is usually a short trip (if any at all) and a smaller distraction for NFL players, while it's often a longer trip and a potentially bigger distraction for college players.

3-NFL players are older and have much more experience. This may contribute to a greater ability to stay focused and well rested during time off and bye weeks.

4-NFL players are also financially stable. In 2011, the minimum NFL player salary was $375,000 (http://www.get2theleague.com/money/average-nfl-player-salary-to-increase-in-2011-season). To contrast this, many college football players attend school on a scholarship and come from families that could be quite poor. The holiday season can be a difficult time for people struggling with finances. This is something that can affect college players that cannot affect NFL players unless they have seriously misspent their minimum $375,000 a year salary. Also, keep in mind that the $375,000 is the bare minimum; it does not include signing bonuses, performance incentives, or endorsements. The average NFL salary in 2011 is $1.9 million dollars (Joe Dorish, Yahoo Sports, http://sports.yahoo.com/nba/news?slug=ycn-10423863). I don't know about you, but nearly $2 million dollars a year is a *little* more than what I was making at my part-time job back in college.

Financial worries are one of the chief reasons for divorce, stress, and even suicide. This concern should be taken seriously in weighing the distraction of a month off the game field, especially during the holiday season. For some of these athletes, their potential professional football career may be their family's only hope of getting out of financial ruin. Think about that pressure for a month with no games to distract you, and see if it doesn't cause some focus problems. Yes, part of being a true star athlete is being able to focus on the game no matter what is going on off the field, but that can be a lot to ask of an 18-22 year-old who has a family in dire financial need.

SHOULD A TEAM THAT CAN'T WIN THEIR CONFERENCE EVEN BE IN THE NATIONAL CHAMPIONSHIP?

That's a hard question to answer. Unfortunately for the BCS and college football as a whole, it is a very valid question. It's just one more example of how the ranking system is a travesty, and it's one more situation that could be avoided by setting up a playoff system. If Alabama was 2nd in their conference but made it to the big game by beating the competition in the playoffs, then there is no controversy. They would have earned their position and proven that they deserved to be there. It is theoretically possible for the best 2 teams in college football to be in the same conference, but that needs to be proven, not speculated.

The subject of a playoff system and the flaws in the current ranking system is a many faceted one, and it's been covered well in other places. There's also the issue of having an all-SEC title game. That's another hot topic that gets a lot of people fighting mad. But for the purpose of this discussion, let's focus on Alabama and whether they are indeed the most deserving team to face LSU in the National Championship.

1. Alabama poses a serious threat, and they have clearly demonstrated this when the teams met in the regular season. They are the only team to truly have threatened to defeat LSU late in the game. And, if any opposing coach knows LSU and has a chance to beat them, it's Nick Saban. He's a former Tigers head coach, and he's been coaching LSU's chief rival, The Crimson Tide, since 2007. It's doubtful that anyone's watched more film on LSU over the last 5 seasons than Saban.

2. Alabama is indeed a fantastic team. Anyone who says otherwise is unfamiliar with their stats. As discussed earlier in this chapter, while LSU boasts slightly better numbers than Alabama, the margin is very slim. One field goal could easily decide this game, as it did when the teams met previously. Alabama's only loss came at the hands of LSU, and one could argue that had the Crimson Tide played anyone else besides LSU, that there would be 2 unbeaten teams in the National Championship. While LSU did beat 8 ranked teams in

2011, Alabama beat 4 ranked teams, and that is no small accomplishment.

3. In 12 games, Alabama beat their opponents by 326 points. That's hard to argue with.

However, the strongest argument against Alabama deserving to face LSU belongs to fans of the Oklahoma State Cowboys. Alabama's record against ranked teams is 4-1, while Oklahoma's record is 5-0. It is true that Oklahoma never had to face LSU, but it is also true that Alabama already had a chance at the Tigers and lost. That does sound awfully convincing in favor of the Cowboys.

The Oklahoma State Cowboys scored 592 points and allowed 310 points in 2011. While 592 offensive points is extremely impressive, especially next to Alabama's 432 points scored, the Cowboys only beat their opponents by 282 points, while the Crimson Tide beat their opponents by 326. The big difference between the teams is Alabama's defense. Alabama only allowed 106 points, while Oklahoma State allowed *nearly 3 times* that amount with 310. Alabama's 8.8 points-allowed-per-game makes Oklahoma State's 25.8 points-allowed-per-game seem a bit ridiculous. There is no doubt that Oklahoma has the better offense, but Alabama's defense is *SO* much better that they've been chosen as #2 in the county.

How much better is Alabama's defense than Oklahoma's offense?

To put it in perspective, for Oklahoma State's offense to be as far ahead of Alabama as Alabama's D is as far ahead of Oklahoma State, Oklahoma would have needed to score 1,263 points in 2011. *Wow*. Yeah, that's a wow stat.

Why isn't Oklahoma State playing against LSU in the National Championship?

Short Answer: The Cowboys' defense blew it. The Cowboys are a fantastic team and would have provided a great opponent for LSU or anyone else, but their lackluster defense is clearly what made Alabama a better choice.

While The Cowboys' explosive offense is very capable of providing a more exciting matchup than a repeat of the defensive trench-fighting in the LSU-Alabama regular season matchup, entertainment has never been the measuring stick for football championships. If excitement is going to be a measure by which teams are selected for the big game, it should be written down in the rulebooks, explaining how it will be judged.

Like I said, the Cowboys could very well be the more exciting opponent for LSU, but if that is to be a deciding factor, coaches need to know that before the start of a season so they can plan their game strategies accordingly in an attempt to make it to the title game based on the new criteria.

The other nail in Oklahoma State's coffin is that they lost to an unranked team, while Alabama lost to the #1-ranked team in the country.

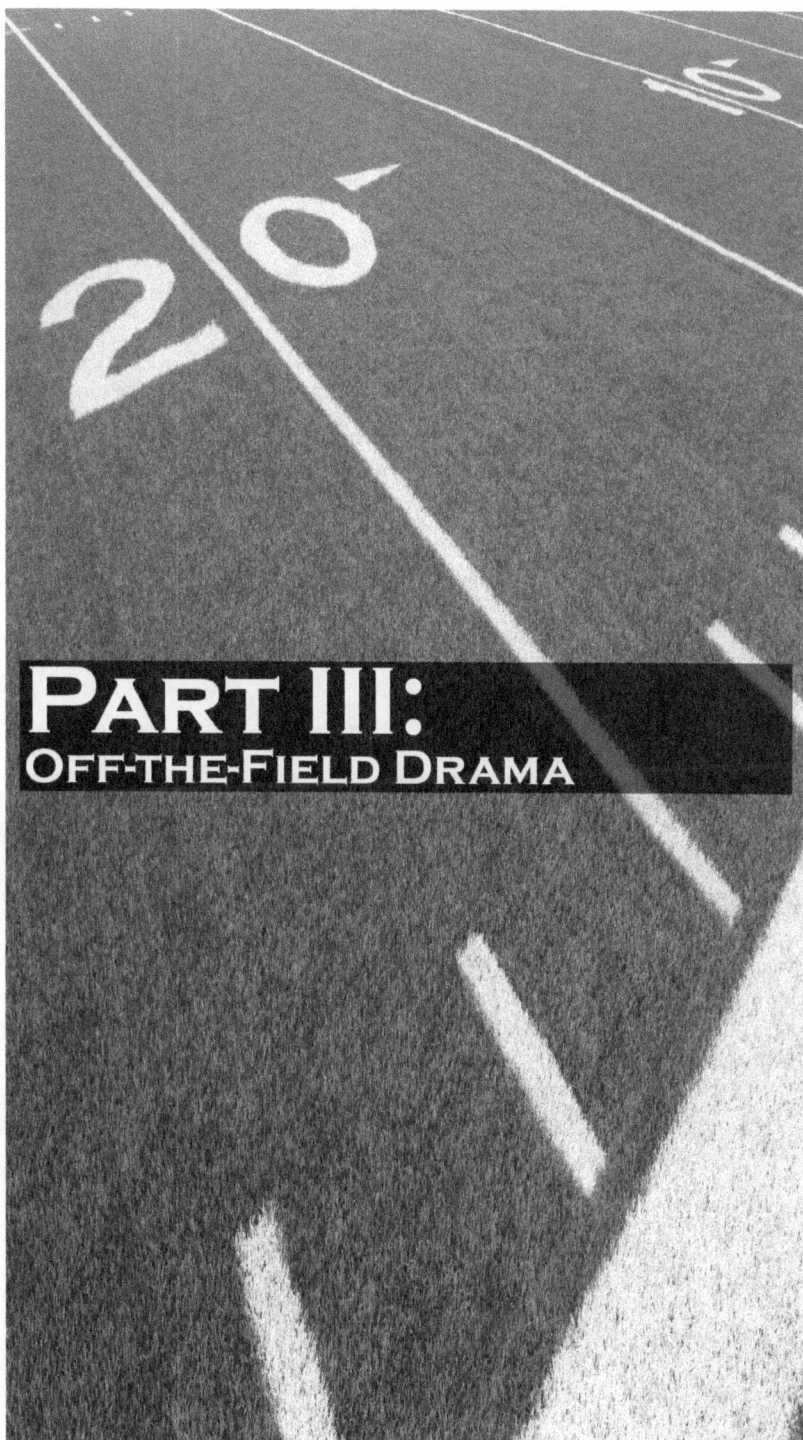

PART III:
OFF-THE-FIELD DRAMA

The first serious challenge facing the 2011 LSU Tigers did not come from the football field. In fact it came from a very unlikely place: outside of Shady's Bar in Tigerland at around 2:00 in the morning.

Some members of LSU's football team were involved in a fight in the bar parking lot. Four people were taken to the hospital after the altercation, none of them football players. The most disturbing allegation was that starting quarterback Jordan Jefferson had kicked a man in the head while he was on the ground. Andrew Lowery, a Marine Reservist, allegedly suffered a broken bone beneath his nose after being kicked by Jefferson, and another man suffered a fractured vertebrae.

On Saturday August 20th, the LSU Tiger Unity Council held a press conference apologizing for the team's actions related to the bar fight and acknowledging that certain members of the team had snuck out and broken their 10:30 p.m. curfew on Thursday August 18th.

Coach Les Miles said, "The last couple of days have been miserable for us. We have been involved in behavior that has been unacceptable to me and our team. Guys have broken team rules and violated team curfew."

In addition to Coach Miles's statement, LSU athletic director, Joe Alleva, said, "We will not tolerate student-athletes whose irresponsible actions tarnish the good name of a great university. LSU student-athletes are expected to behave with the understanding that they represent their school, their fellow students, and the long history of this program, regardless of the time of day.

"Coach Miles has already begun taking disciplinary action. It is critical that we are deliberate in determining the facts surrounding this incident, and as Coach Miles said, when the facts are clear, additional and appropriate disciplinary action will be taken, if necessary."

("LSU's Miles says players' behavior 'unacceptable." Glenn Guilbeau. August 20,2011. *USA Today*.
http://www.usatoday.com/sports/college/football/sec/2011-08-20-lsu-les-miles_n.htm)

On August 26, 2011, LSU suspended the athletes involved. The real weight of the suspension and the worry for LSU fans was that the players were not just suspended for a game or two, but they were suspended indefinitely. That could easily have meant the entire season, or even that the players would never return to the team, especially if they found themselves in a high-profile trial or serving jail time.

Also on August 26th, Jordan Jefferson was arrested by Baton Rouge police for second-degree battery which is a felony. After two days of testimony, Jefferson's charges were dropped to simple battery, which is a misdemeanor. Soon after that, he was reinstated to the team.

On October 3rd at a weekly press luncheon, Les Miles commented on the fans booing when Jefferson was put into that weekend's game:

"Jordan Jefferson didn't have a choice. I sent him in the game, OK. And when he went into the game, he'd already served a four-game suspension. He'd been through quite a lot. And it appears to me that this thing's going to be a misdemeanor. Not unlike a lot of the people in the stands who possibly had similar run-ins with the law, okay. Well, I suspect that they didn't get penalized nearly as significantly as this guy."

Unapologetic, Jordan Jefferson had this to say, "I don't regret anything. God puts people in certain situations for a reason. He's the only person that can control my destiny. He's the only person that knows my future. There was judgment from a lot of people. The only person that can judge me in this world is God. I don't regret any of the pain that I've been through. I don't regret anything that has happened to me. I don't regret the situation that I have been in. I learned a lot from that situation."

When asked if he apologized to his team, Jefferson said, "I mean, I talked to the team throughout the whole process. I mean, I didn't have to apologize because we all were there (laughs). So I didn't have to apologize for anything."

When asked about his replacement in backup quarterback Jarrett Lee, Jefferson said, "I've been supporting Jarrett throughout the whole year. He's done a great job on the field, led the troops to victory. That's what we're trained to do, and he has been doing a great job of that."

("LSU's Jefferson isn't apologetic, wants to start again" Glenn Guilbeau. October 4, 2011
http://www.usatoday.com/sports/college/football/sec/story/2011-10-03/lsu-quarterback-jordan-jefferson-not-apologetic/50649980/1)

As if the bar fight was not enough drama for the 2011 Tigers, three players were suspended for testing positive for synthetic marijuana. The players were team-leading rusher, Spencer Ware; cornerback, Tyrann Mathieu; and defensive back, Tharold Simon. All 3 of these key players were suspended from the Auburn game.

If there is a silver lining to these negative and embarrassing setbacks, it is that LSU rose above them and won every single game of the season. The team remained focused and did what they needed to do on the football field.

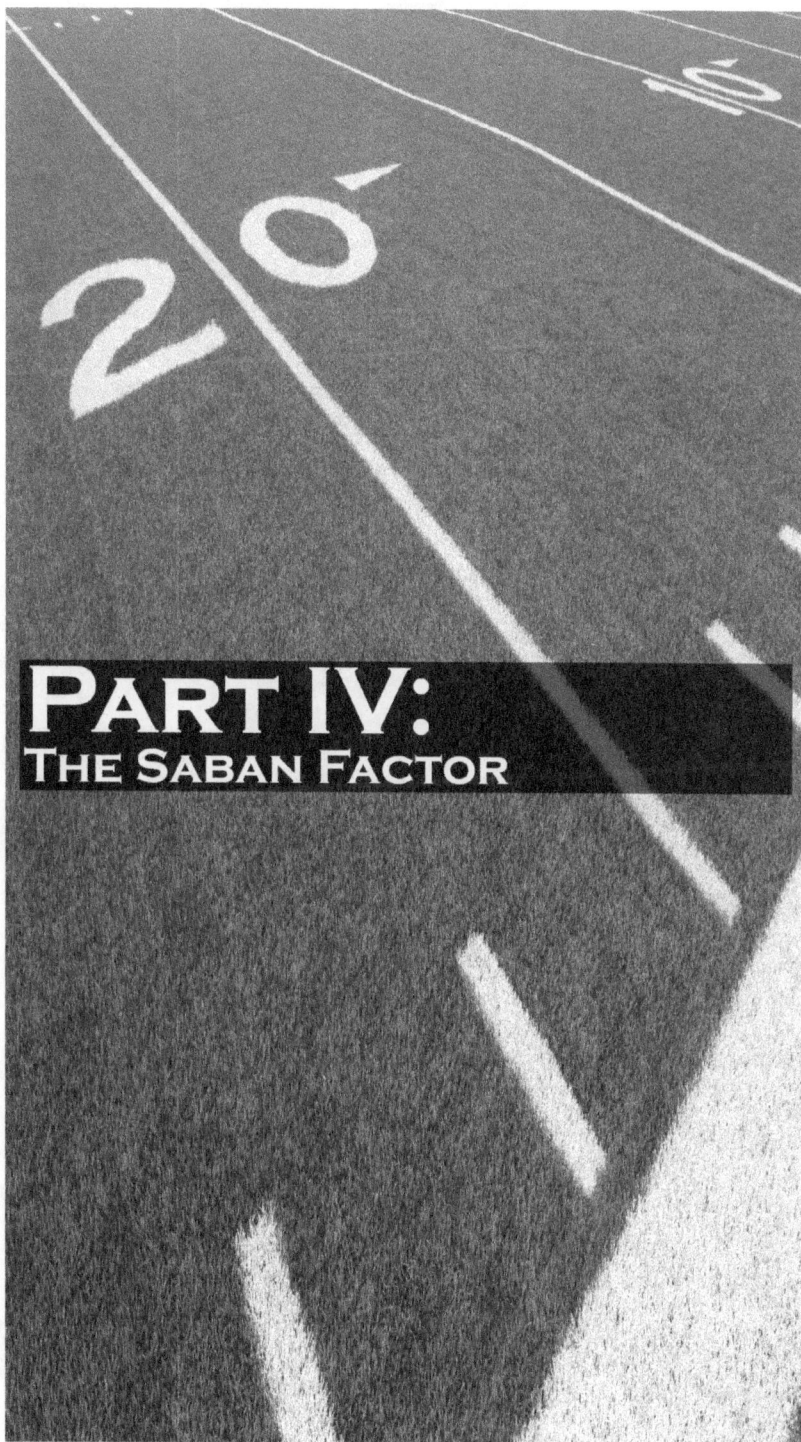

PART IV:
THE SABAN FACTOR

THE SABAN FACTOR
AN OLD FRIEND & A NEW ENEMY

O kay, so the chapter title may be a little dramatic, but it does somewhat capture the long-standing relationship between Nick Saban and LSU fans.

A little history...

Nick Saban took over head coaching duties at LSU from Gary DiNardo for the 2000 football season. Despite getting fans' hopes up on several occasions, DiNardo could never get the Tigers into championship shape, and in his last year with the team, he led them to an uninspired 3-8 record.

In just his first year as head coach, Saban improved LSU's record to 8-4. He basically flipped their record around, turning the Tigers from a team that lost nearly three times as much as they won into a team that won twice as much as they lost.

In his second year in Baton Rouge, Saban coached LSU to win an SEC championship. In only two years' time, the Tigers went from a 3-8 record to SEC Champions. That's pretty amazing.

The crowning achievement of Saban's tenure at LSU was obviously the 2003 shared National Championship.

Saban stayed on for one more year following the national championship, leading the Tigers to a 9-3 season, which included a heart-wrenching 1-point loss to Auburn.

When Saban left college football to coach in the NFL's 2005 season, he did not leave LSU for rival Alabama. He became the head coach of the Miami Dolphins. The last two sentences are extremely obvious, but they deserve repeating, because some people seem to think that Saban did indeed leave LSU for Alabama, and that is downright silly. The simple truth is that while Saban eventually left the Miami Dolphins to become Alabama's head coach, his job was not guaranteed with the Dolphins' disappointing 6-10 2006 Season. Any NFL coach with a 6-10 record is in danger of losing his job, especially a high profile coach who has not performed up to expectations. If the 2007 season did not show significant improvement for the Dolphins, Saban would very likely have been fired, harming both his reputation and the salary that he could receive elsewhere. For the record, the 2007 Dolphins were plagued with problems on and off the field which led to a miserable 1-15 season. Three Dolphins players were arrested that year, and one can only speculate if these personnel problems were an additional motivation for Saban to seek a new position.

In January of 2007, Alabama needed a coach, and Saban needed/wanted a new coaching job. Seeking work in one's qualified field is not a malicious act. If LSU had offered Saban his job back for the same money that Alabama offered and Saban had then refused LSU to go to Alabama, then, one could argue ill will and a lack of loyalty, but that didn't happen. The man wanted to return to college football and took the best position available at the time.

Seriously, folks...
Sometimes as sports fans, we need a good head check every now and then. Heading into a hyped-up LSU-Alabama rematch for bragging rights to being the best college football team in the nation, it may be time for a little head check.

So, what head check might LSU fans need going into the BCS Championship Game versus Alabama and even into upcoming seasons?

Head Check 1 - Simple, Common Sense

Opposing teams are fellow competitors, not dire enemies. Fans of the opposing team are not inherently all jerks, and even athletes and coaches on the opposing team are not all cheaters and terrible people. This is nothing new, but some fans can forget these simple facts and a problem can develop when they become passionate *beyond reason*. When this happens, friendly competition and ribbing can easily turn nasty, insulting, and even hostile. Therefore, the above is always worth keeping in mind. This is general sports stuff and does not apply specifically to this game or LSU/Alabama fans, but it applies to all sports. And, as long as there are drunken fights in the stands and snarky, mean-spirited fanboys spewing vitriol all over ESPN and NFL forums, it bears repeating.

Head Check 2: Nick Saban does not hate the LSU Tigers or LSU Fans.

Where is the proof of this? It's in Nick Saban's own words.

WHEN ASKED IF HE TALKS TO LES MILES:

"Yeah, I talk to Coach Miles all the time. **I like Coach Miles. I think he's done a wonderful job, and what he's done at LSU since he's been there.** Obviously, you know, he has a great team this year that he's done a fantastic job with. It's hard to go undefeated now. It's hard to go undefeated in our league…He's done just a great job. And we've done several other things together. **I have a lot of respect and admiration for what [Les Miles] he's done and who he is.** We talk on occasion about SEC issues and problems and college football in general in the future."

(Nick Saban, press conference on December 19, 2011)
Al.com. 19 December 2011.
<http://www.al.com/sports/index.ssf/2011/12/nick_saban_talks_alabama_lsu_a.html>

ON LOUISIANA FOOTBALL PLAYERS & HIS SUCCESS ON RECRUITING LOUISIANA PLAYERS:

"We do have several very good players on our team from Louisiana...guys that have done extremely well for us. There [sic] is **a lot of good players in Louisiana.** There is a lot of great high school football in Louisiana. They [LSU] have a lot of good players on their team from Louisiana. And we are pleased and happy with the job that the guys that we have from Louisiana [sic] has done for us."
(Nick Saban, press conference on November 2, 2011)
Al.com. 2 November 2011.
<http://www.al.com/sports/index.ssf/2011/12/nick_saban_talks_alabama_lsu
_a.html >

ON PLAYING LSU IN THE REGULAR SEASON:

"...with **total respect** for the people that you're playing against, because they're [LSU] very good for a reason...We have a lot of respect for this team...as well as what they've been able to accomplish as a team. Les Miles has done a fabulous job there of not only of recruiting a lot of very talented players, but doing a very good job of developing those players and being able to execute and have a lot of success in all three phases of the game: offense, defense and special teams; they're very, very good. And **it doesn't take long to see why they are an undefeated team**...They have two good quarterbacks...guys that are very capable of beating you in terms of what they do well...They've been able to run the ball effectively...Defensively, they are in the top 5 in just about every category...They're a very, very good defensive team. And I think they're first in our league in special teams...**This [LSU] is a very, very good team all the way around.**"

(Nick Saban, press conference on October 31, 2011)
Al.com. 31 October 2011.
<http://www.al.com/sports/index.ssf/2011/12/nick_saban_talks_alabama_lsu
_a.html >

In summary, Saban has publicly complimented Les Miles as a coach and a person, Louisiana as a football state, and the 2011 LSU Tigers as being a great team in every category.

Strictly speaking, hating Nick Saban is also hating the success of the 2000-2004 LSU Tigers, who achieved a 48–16 record and a shared 2003 National Championship. However, there is nothing wrong with a healthy rivalry, the key word being *healthy*. What better rivalry could there be than beating a long-term rival, the Alabama Crimson Tide, coached by former coach Nick Saban? There's nothing wrong with that, but that doesn't make Saban a bad person.

When Bobby Hebert and Morten Andersen left the New Orleans Saints for rival Atlanta Falcons, it didn't undo the good things that these fan-favorites did for the long-suffering Saints. The Bobby Hebert/Morten Andersen era produced the *first winning seasons ever* for the Saints, but they did both leave the Saints and play for the Falcons. Bobby Hebert is now back home in Louisiana and is the voice of the Saints on local radio. His playing for another team, even a fierce rival, did not destroy his love for the Saints or his home. Coincidentally, Saints fans are typically also LSU Tigers fans, so this is particularly relevant to them.

CONCLUSION:

A healthy, heated rivalry?
That's perfectly acceptable and possibly even beneficial to the game.

Feeling like you want to physically harm a former coach who led your favorite team to the BCS Championship just 9 years ago?
It's time for a time out and a head check.

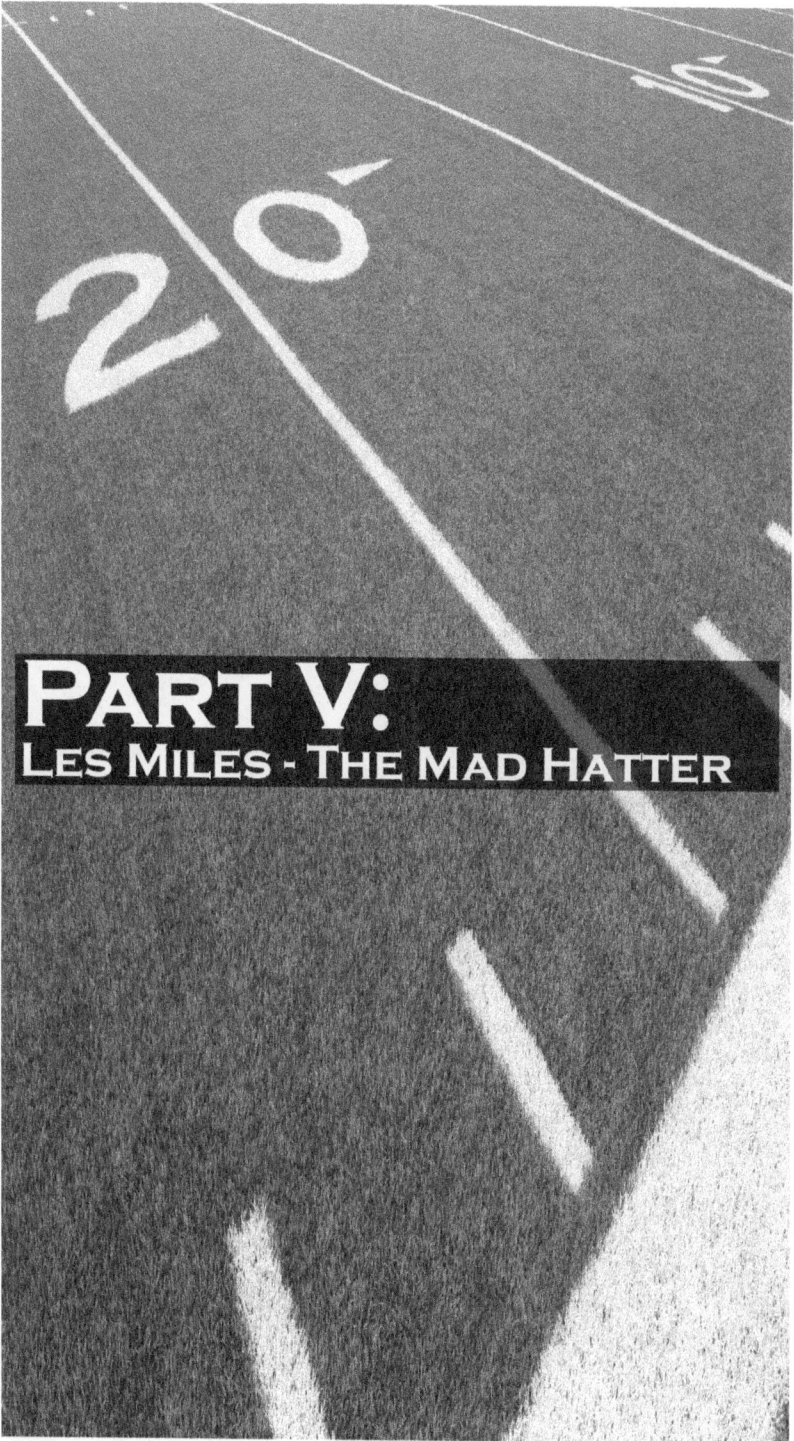

PART V:
LES MILES - THE MAD HATTER

LES MILES
THE MAD HATTER

L es Miles is lovingly known as The Mad Hatter to the college football world. He's known for being inventive and unorthodox, a coach that is always thinking and will fight until the last second of the 4th quarter, no matter what the score may be.

As a high school athlete, Miles played baseball, wrestling, and football, lettering in all 3 sports and earning all-state selection in the latter. While attending the University of Michigan, he became a 2-year football letterman. A few years later, Miles came back to Michigan to become an assistant football coach.

Miles's 1st head-coaching job came with Oklahoma State, and after having one losing season, he led them to 3 winning seasons and 3 bowl appearances. During this time, Miles was named the 2002 Big 12 Conference Coach of the Year by the Associated Press.

When Nick Saban left LSU for the NFL via the Miami Dolphins, LSU was looking for a remarkable coach to replace him and continue the Tigers recent and remarkable success. They found just the coach in Les Miles who came to Baton Rouge as the Tigers' 32nd head coach.

If he already did not have enough pressure taking over the Tigers who had recently won a National Championship and were expected to compete for the title again, Hurricane Katrina hit Louisiana in August 2005 before the 1st game of the season. Despite all of the challenges, Miles coached LSU to an 11-2 record and a Peach Bowl victory over the Miami Hurricanes.

In 2006, the Tigers went 10-2, giving LSU their first back-to-back 10-win seasons in school history. The season ended with LSU pounding Notre Dame in the Sugar Bowl 41-14.

The 2007 season was an interesting one for several reasons. First, this season displayed some of Miles's more unorthodox play-calling. Second, LSU was ranked #1 on two different occasions during the season. Thirdly, LSU lost two upset games to #17 Kentucky and to Arkansas, who was unranked. The Arkansas game was a puzzling and high-scoring loss with a score of 50-48. In a baffling coincidence, both losses came in triple overtime. Triple overtime upset losses might be the hardest defeats for fans to take, so that made parts of the year a little difficult for Tigers supporters. However, LSU still went on to the SEC Championship Game and defeated Tennessee 21-14. The victory was not the most interesting news for LSU that day.

It was rumored twice that Les Miles was going to leave LSU to take a head coaching position at his alma mater, Michigan. On the day of the SEC Championship Game, ESPN *College GameDay* reporter, Kirk Herbstreit, erroneously stated that Les Miles had decided to go back to his alma mater and accepted the job of the new University of Michigan Head Football Coach. If anything can throw off a team before a championship game, it's hearing just before the game starts that your head coach is leaving you for another college.

And to make the day even more bizarre, #1 Missouri and #2 West Virginia *BOTH* lost their games, which moved the Tigers very unexpectedly into the #2 spot. LSU went on to beat Ohio State in the BCS National Championship Game with a score of 38-24. This granted the 12-2 Tigers the National Championship, which was Les Miles' first and only the third in LSU history.

A press conference was immediately held, and Les Miles announced:

"There was some misinformation on ESPN and I think it's imperative that I straighten it out. I am the head coach at LSU. I will be the head coach at LSU. I have no interest in talking to anybody else. I've got a championship game to play, and I am excited about the opportunity of my damn strong football team to play in it. That's really all I'd like to say. It was unfortunate that I had to address my team with this information this morning. With that being done, I think we'd be ready to play. There will be no questions for me. I represent me in this issue. Please ask me after. I'm busy. Thank you very much. Have a great day."

("This Is The Place I Want To Be." *The Advocate.* 2 December 2007 http://www.2theadvocate.com/sports/lsu/12026681.html)

Despite that clear statement, rumors still persisted that Miles was indeed considering the job or had already secretly accepted the job for the next season. To that Miles responded again:

"I'm going to be the coach at LSU next season."

("Miles: 'I'll say it again, I'm going to be the coach at LSU'" ESPN College Football December 11, 2007 http://sports.espn.go.com/ncf/news/story?id=3150159)

Thankfully for LSU fans, Les was telling the truth. The 2008 season proved to be a bit of a disappointed to fans, but it was still a winning season with an 8-5 record and a win in the *Chick-Fil-A* Bowl.

2009 and 2010 were also winning seasons with trips to the Capital One and Cotton Bowls.

All in all, Les Miles has amassed an incredible 75-17 record at LSU. His statistics truly speak for his ability as a coach and for his dedication to the Tigers.

Les Miles Head Coaching Record

Season	College	Record	Bowl Game
2001	Oklahoma State	04-07	N/A
2002	Oklahoma State	08-05	**WIN - Houston**
2003	Oklahoma State	09-04	*LOSS - Cotton*
2004	Oklahoma State	07-05	*LOSS – Alamo*
2005	LSU	11-2	**WIN – Chick-Fil-A**
2006	LSU	11-2	**WIN – Sugar**
2007	LSU	12-2	**WIN – BCS**
2008	LSU	8-5	**WIN - Chick-Fil-A**
2009	LSU	9-4	*LOSS – Capital One*
2010	LSU	11-2	**WIN – Cotton**
2011	LSU	13-0	**BCS**
ALL	**ALL**	**103-38**	

Les Miles Oklahoma Head Coaching Record

Seasons	College	Record	Win %	Bowl Game Record
2001-2004	Oklahoma State	28-21	57 %	1-2

Les Miles LSU Head Coaching Record

Seasons	College	Record	Win %	Bowl Game Record
2005-2011	LSU	75-17	81.5 %	5-1 (not including 2011 BCS)

CHECK OUT MORE GREAT RELEASES FROM
MEGALODON ENTERTAINMENT LLC

ISBN 978-0-9800605-7-7